DOES A GIRAFFE DRIVE?

Fred Ehrlich, M.D.
Pictures by Emily Bolam

🍎 Blue Apple Books
Maplewood, N.J.

Text copyright © 2007 by Fred Ehrlich
Illustrations copyright © 2007 by Emily Bolam
All rights reserved   CIP Data is available.
First published in the United States 2007 by
🍎 Blue Apple Books
515 Valley Street, Maplewood, N.J. 07040
www.blueapplebooks.com

Distributed in the U.S. by Chronicle Books
First Edition Printed in China

ISBN 13: 978-1-59354-614-4
ISBN 10: 1-59354-614-9

1 3 5 7 9 10 8 6 4 2

Does a giraffe drive?

No!

Giraffes walk, using both right legs, then both left legs, so their long limbs don't get tangled.

When giraffes gallop, their back legs go outside their front legs to prevent them from tripping and falling.

Does a donkey drive?

No way!

Donkeys walk, run, or gallo
but a donkey doesn't drive

A donkey can pull a cart.
But it needs a driver to tell it
where to go and when to stop.

Does a cheetah drive?

What a silly idea!

A cheetah is the fastest animal on land.
A cheetah can run faster than a man or a woman.
It can even run faster than some trucks.

Spider monkeys can walk
on all fours.

They can climb and swing in trees
using their hands and feet.

They can stand on their hind feet
and leap from one tree to another.
But monkeys do not drive . . .

or fly like birds . . .

or swim
like fish.

People cannot fly like birds.
People cannot swim as well as fish.

People cannot gallop like horses
or run as fast as cheetahs.

All animals move, but only people are smart
enough to invent ways to help them move
faster and better over longer distances.

To cross rivers, streams and oceans,
people made rafts,

canoes,

small rowboats,

ships with sails,

and big boats with motors.

So that they could travel across the land better
and carry things with them,
people used their brains to make:

carts

wagons

trucks

cars

trains

But people really wanted to fly.

First they went up
in the air in big,
hot-air balloons.

Then came
the first small airplane,
which stayed in the air
for 12 seconds.

Many people worked together over many years to figure out how a plane could fly people over long distances.

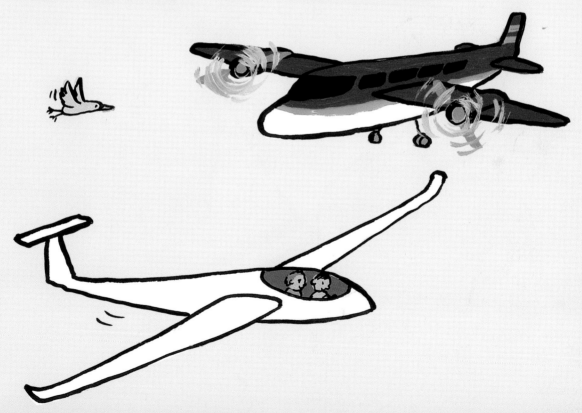

People are always
using their brains to think
of new ways to get places.

What do you think will come next